The Power of Habit

The Power of Habit

MASTERING THE ART OF
PRODUCTIVITY

B. Vincent

QuillQuest Publishers

Contents

Introduction   1

1   Chapter 1: Understanding Habits   5

2   Chapter 2: The Habit Loop - Decoding the Path to Productivity   10

3   Chapter 3: Keystone Habits: The Cornerstones of Success   15

4   Chapter 4: The Role of Belief in Habit Change   21

5   Chapter 5: The Golden Rule of Habit Change   27

6   Chapter 6: The Habit of Productivity   33

7   Chapter 7: Overcoming Obstacles to Habit Change   39

8   Chapter 8: Habit Stacking and Compound Growth   45

Conclusion   51

Appendix   56

Introduction

The Meaning of Propensities

At the center of each and every activity we take lies a propensity ready to be perceived. Propensities are the undetectable design of our regular routines, quietly directing our ways of behaving, molding our decisions, and, at last, directing the course of our reality. They are the strings that weave the texture of our personality, our schedules, and our accomplishments. Understanding the job of propensities isn't just about perceiving the examples of our activities; it's tied in with getting a handle on the significant effect these robotized ways of behaving have on our lives.

Each propensity, from the second we wake to the contemplations that float through our psyches around evening time, consolidates to make the mosaic of our everyday experience. These propensities can lift us higher than ever of accomplishment or drive us into the profundities of despondency. They are strong in light of the fact that they are many times inconspicuous, working behind the scenes, impacting our choices without our cognizant mindfulness. It's exclusively by exposing these propensities, analyzing their design and reason, that we can start to tackle their power.

The meaning of propensities stretches out past individual activities; they are the structure blocks of cultural standards and societies. Our aggregate propensities shape the social orders we live in, the economies we take part in, and the set of experiences we compose. On an individual level, understanding the idea of our propensities is the most important move towards significant individual change. By improving on our propensities, we transform us.

The excursion through this book is an investigation of how propensities structure, how they can be reshaped, and how, by dominating them, we can open the way to turning out to be more useful, satisfied, and enabled people. The mission to comprehend and further develop our propensities isn't just about making outside proportions of progress; it's tied in with taking advantage of our idle potential, finding our inward assets, and understanding that, inside the domain of our propensities, lies the ability to shape our predetermination.

Points and Construction of the Book

This book is planned as a compass for exploring the territory of individual change through the dominance of propensities. Its essential point is to outfit you with the information and devices important to change your propensities, and likewise, your life. Through the pages that follow, you will set out on an excursion that goes past simple hypothetical investigation; you will find viable, significant techniques that can be applied to your day to day schedules, guaranteeing enduring changes and a more useful life.

To direct you on this excursion, the book is organized into cautiously organized parts, each zeroing in on a particular part of propensity development, change, and enhancement. The underlying sections establish the groundwork, acquainting you with the fundamental ideas of propensity development and the science hidden these cycles. As the story advances, we dig further into procedures for recognizing, destroying, and modifying propensities, with an emphasis on upgrading efficiency and accomplishing individual objectives.

Also, the book accentuates the groundbreaking force of cornerstone propensities and their far reaching influences on different everyday issues. It investigates the mental parts of propensity change, remembering the job of conviction and local area for working with feasible change. Viable guidance on defeating snags and utilizing the compound impacts of little propensity changes offers a guide to a more focused and satisfying life.

By organizing the book along these lines, I want to not just furnish you with a comprehension of the mechanics of propensities yet in addition to offer a bit by bit guide that can be custom-made to accommodate your own conditions and desires. This isn't simply a book to be perused; it is an asset to be utilized, a buddy on your excursion towards excelling at efficiency through the impact of trained instinct.

The Science Behind Propensities

Propensities, as we've come to comprehend, are undeniably more than simple redundancies of conduct; they are well established in the brain connections of our cerebrums. This segment of the book moves back the drape on the intriguing universe of propensity development and have an impact on according to a logical viewpoint, revealing insight into why we do what we do and how we can modify our direction.

At the core of propensity arrangement lies the cerebrum's ability to stagger to streamline its tasks. At the point when a way of behaving is rehashed, our minds search for ways of saving exertion by changing over the succession of activities into a programmed daily practice, an interaction known as "piecing." This proficiency is pivotal for our endurance, permitting us to concentrate on clever dangers and open doors. Notwithstanding, it's this very cycle that can make propensities, both great and terrible, challenging to break once they are solidly settled.

Understanding the propensity circle — containing a signal, a daily practice, and a prize — offers us an outline for change. The sign triggers the way of behaving, the routine is the actual conduct, and the prize lets our mind know that the routine merits recalling. It's a circle that, once started, can turn nearly without exertion, yet with information and aim, can be overhauled.

Neuroscientific research has shown that while propensities might be profoundly instilled, the cerebrum's versatility implies that they are not unchanging. Each time we play out a propensity, we fortify the brain associations related with that way of behaving. On the other hand, when we change our everyday practice because of the prompt, regardless accomplish a remunerating result, we start to produce new pathways. This book use these experiences, introducing them in a way that isn't just open yet in addition pragmatic, offering a guide for bridling the cerebrum's versatility to roll out enduring improvements.

By demystifying the science behind propensities, this book means to enable you with the information that change isn't just imaginable yet attainable. With this getting it, you can move toward the errand of changing your propensities with certainty, furnished with systems that are grounded in a profound comprehension of how our minds work.

1

∽

Chapter 1: Understanding Habits

Characterizing Propensities: The Essential Parts

At the core of our day to day activities and schedules lie propensities, the programmed reactions that direct quite a bit of our way of behaving without the requirement for cognizant idea. To really comprehend the idea of propensities, analyzing them into their fundamental parts: the signal, the daily schedule, and the reward is fundamental. This structure works on the idea of propensities as well as uncovers the instrument behind their development and perseverance over the long haul.

The Prompt fills in as the trigger for the propensity, starting the grouping of activities that follow. It very well may be anything from a period of day, a specific close to home state, or any sort of tactile sign that advises our mind to go into programmed mode and which propensity to utilize.

The Routine is the actual conduct, the activity we take naturally when we experience the sign. This can go from proactive tasks like snatching some espresso the second we awaken, to mental or close to home schedules, for example, checking virtual entertainment while feeling exhausted or desolate.

The Prize is the explanation the mind recollects this specific circle from here on out; it's the advantage or fulfillment we gain from playing

5

out the everyday practice. The prize can be anything that our mind sees as pleasurable or valuable, supporting the propensity circle by guaranteeing that the cerebrum focuses on its maintenance for sometime later.

Understanding these parts is much the same as holding a guide when you're lost; it offers clearness and bearing. By ending down propensities into these basic parts, we can begin to investigate our own ways of behaving, recognize what parts are adding to undesirable propensities, and start the most common way of rolling out purposeful improvements. This part lays the basis for that excursion, giving the devices important to decipher the intricate snare of propensities that impact our lives. From this perspective, we're equipped for understanding our propensities as well as ready to dominate them, making way for the groundbreaking excursion that lies ahead.

The Mind and Propensity Arrangement

The development of propensities isn't simply an issue of self control or moral strength; it's well established in the multifaceted operations of the human cerebrum. This understanding is significant, as it moves the story from one of individual inability to a more merciful and logical point of view on conduct change. The mind, continuously looking to upgrade its capabilities, assumes a focal part in propensity development, transforming successive activities into programmed schedules to save energy for additional requesting undertakings.

At the point when we more than once participate in a way of behaving that is set off by a particular signal and followed by a remunerating sensation, our cerebrum begins to connect these components together, framing a brain process that makes the activity simpler and more proficient to perform over the long haul. This cycle, known as 'lumping,' permits complex successions of activities to be done with negligible cognizant information, opening up mental assets for different exercises. It's the reason we can end up at our objective without recollecting the drive or enjoy a nibble without cognizant navigation.

Understanding this brain premise of propensity arrangement enlightens why propensities can be so versatile to change. When a way of behaving becomes programmed, the brain processes related with it are fortified, making the propensity a default reaction to its prompt. This doesn't mean, notwithstanding, that change is unimaginable. The cerebrum's pliancy guarantees that new pathways can be fashioned and reinforced over the long run, offering expect those hoping to bring an end to liberated from pointless propensities.

This section of the book digs into the neurological cycles behind propensity development, giving a strong groundwork to the techniques examined in later parts. By grasping how propensities are wired into our cerebrums, we can move toward the assignment of adjusting them with more prominent adequacy and understanding, utilizing designated techniques that line up with the mind's intrinsic systems of progress.

The Pervasiveness of Propensities in Day to day existence

Propensities, frequently working underneath the edge of our cognizant mindfulness, assume a stupendous part in chiseling our day to day routines. They are the concealed modelers of our schedules, unobtrusively directing the cadence of our days, from the second we wake until we shut our eyes around evening time. This segment investigates the unavoidable impact of propensities, showing how they form our activities as well as our discernments, choices, and cooperations with our general surroundings.

Each part of our everyday presence, from the unremarkable to the significant, is pervaded by propensities. The manner in which we clean our teeth, the course we take to work, how we answer messages, and even the way that we loosen up at night — are completely administered by scholarly schedules. These propensities structure a perplexing web that shapes our proficiency, efficiency, and in general prosperity. They can move us towards our objectives or, alternately, go about as obstructions to our advancement.

The force of propensities reaches out past individual activities, impacting our aggregate ways of behaving and cultural standards. The ceremonies we notice, the items we consume, and the social decorums we follow are appearances of shared propensities, woven into the texture of our way of life and society. Perceiving the pervasiveness of propensities in day to day existence is urgent, as it highlights the effect of our programmed ways of behaving on the more extensive range of our reality.

By featuring instances of propensities that we could ignore, this segment expects to hone the peruser's consciousness of their own schedules. Understanding the inescapability of propensities is the most important move towards purposeful living. It welcomes us to examine our programmed ways of behaving, to scrutinize their utility, and, at last, to settle on cognizant decisions about which propensities we wish to develop and which we try to change. This enlivening to the omnipresence of propensities fills in as a source of inspiration, encouraging us to assume command over our ways of behaving and, likewise, our lives.

Recognizing Great and Negative behavior patterns

In the multifaceted embroidery of our lives, propensities arise as strings of fluctuating shades, some adding energetic shades of efficiency and energy, while others cast hazier tints of stagnation and weakness. This qualification among "great" and "terrible" propensities, however apparently direct, is profoundly nuanced and innately abstract, contingent upon individual qualities, objectives, and the setting of one's life. This section investigates the division of propensities, giving a structure to assess and adjust our schedules to our most profound goals.

A "great" propensity, basically, is one that pushes us toward our objectives, upgrades our prosperity, and improves our lives. These are the propensities that sustain our wellbeing, reinforce our connections, and enhance our efficiency. They are as one with our qualities and goals, going about as undaunted partners as we continued looking for individual and expert satisfaction.

Alternately, "awful" propensities are those that upset our advancement, hurt our wellbeing, or cheapen our personal satisfaction. They are the schedules that, however maybe offering brief solace or getaway, at last lead us from the existence we want. These propensities frequently emerge from neglected requirements, stress, or the quest for guaranteed satisfaction, and they persevere on the grounds that they satisfy a transient void, notwithstanding their drawn out costs.

The test, then, lies not in that frame of mind as fortunate or unfortunate from a moralistic perspective, however in knowing which propensities serve us and which don't. This requires a sharp familiarity with our qualities, objectives, and the results of our activities. By analyzing the prizes that our propensities bring, we can more readily comprehend their part in our lives and arrive at informed conclusions about which propensities to sustain and which to change.

This segment offers techniques for this acumen interaction, empowering perusers to ponder their propensities from the perspective of their own goals. It recommends techniques for following propensities, assessing their effects, and deliberately picking the schedules that line up with the existence they wish to lead. Through this intelligent practice, we can start to reshape our propensities, guiding them in bearings that improve our prosperity and push us toward our most treasured objectives. This investigation of the nuanced scene of propensities highlights the force of decision and the potential for change inborn in each daily schedule.

2

Chapter 2: The Habit Loop - Decoding the Path to Productivity

Prologue to the Propensity Circle and Its Parts

Section 2 leaves on an excursion into the core of propensity development, presenting the idea of the Propensity Circle — a strong system for understanding and changing our ways of behaving. This circle, a cycle comprising of three key parts: the Sign, the Daily schedule, and the Prize, fills in as the diagram for each propensity we structure, from the harmless to the groundbreaking. Understanding this circle is essential for anybody hoping to saddle the force of propensities to upgrade efficiency and accomplish individual objectives.

The Prompt goes about as the trigger for the propensity, a particular sign that starts the way of behaving. It very well may be anything from a natural brief, like strolling into a dim room and going after the light switch, to a profound express that urges us to search out a specific solace.

The Routine is the actual conduct, the move we make because of the signal. This could go from a basic actual demonstration to a mind boggling succession of ways of behaving, profoundly instilled through redundancy.

The Award is the result, the explanation our mind recollects and esteems this specific arrangement of activities. The prize shuts the circle, making a memory of fulfillment or advantage that captivates us to rehash the conduct in the future when a similar sign is experienced.

By digging into the parts of the Propensity Circle, this section lays the preparation for dismantling and reproducing propensities. It's through the fastidious examination of every component of the circle that we can start to distinguish which parts of our schedules are serving us and which are not. This understanding is the initial step on the way to efficiency, empowering us to decisively alter our propensities to all the more likely line up with our yearnings and targets. Through genuine models and commonsense experiences, we investigate how to distinguish and control every part of the Propensity Circle, making way for significant individual change.

Step by step instructions to Distinguish Your Propensity Circles: Signs, Schedules, and Rewards

With the structure of the Propensity Circle divulged, the subsequent stage on our excursion to dominating efficiency is figuring out how to fastidiously distinguish our own propensity circles. This investigation is similar to turning into a paleontologist of oneself, digging through the layers of our everyday schedules to reveal the signs, schedules, and rewards that drive our way of behaving. This segment is devoted to furnishing you with the instruments and bits of knowledge important to lead this self-assessment, a significant cycle for anybody aim on reshaping their propensities to cultivate a more useful life.

Distinguishing Signals requires sharp perception and reflection. It includes following your ways of behaving and taking note of the natural, profound, or worldly triggers that go before them. Whether seeing your running shoes prompts a morning run or the sensation of stress that prompts a short breather, perceiving these signals is the most important phase in understanding your propensity circles.

Understanding Schedules is tied in with perceiving the moves you naturally make in light of your signs. This step requests trustworthiness and mindfulness, as it's barely noticeable the schedules that have become natural. By recording your activities, regardless of how immaterial they could appear, you start to see the examples of conduct that comprise your everyday existence.

Revealing Prizes includes distinguishing the advantages you accept you get from a propensity. Prizes can be prompt and tactile, similar to the flavor of espresso, or more conceptual, like the liberating sensation from having some time off. Now and again, the prize isn't what it appears to be on a superficial level, and more profound reflection is expected to figure out the genuine result.

This part directs you through pragmatic activities and reflections intended to uncover your propensity circles. By keeping a propensity journal, considering your sentiments and responses, and exploring different avenues regarding changes to your schedules, you can start to translate the intricate trap of ways of behaving that shape your life. This interaction enlightens the design of your propensities as well as engages you to assume command over them, setting a strong starting point for the groundbreaking techniques that follow.

Contextual analyses of Fruitful Propensity Circle Changes

In enlightening the way to dominating our propensities, there is massive worth in gaining from the excursions of others. This part of the book exposes a progression of convincing contextual investigations that feature the significant effect of understanding and modifying propensity circles. Through these stories, we investigate the genuine utilizations of the ideas presented before, giving unmistakable proof of the extraordinary subconscious training circle change.

Each contextual investigation highlights people who, confronted with ineffective schedules and the craving for change, left on the excursion of unraveling their propensity circles. From a Chief battling with dawdling to an essayist doing combating an inability to write, these accounts length a different scope of difficulties and goals. What joins them is the approach applied in recognizing and adjusting the parts of their propensity circles

— signal, everyday practice, and prize — to fashion new ways toward efficiency and satisfaction.

One case features an expert competitor who, by moving the prompts that prompted useless preparation propensities, figured out how to improve his exhibition fundamentally. Another story dives into the existence of a bustling mother who changed her everyday daily schedule by modifying the prize construction of her morning propensities, prompting expanded using time effectively and individual time.

These accounts act as confirmation of idea as well as proposition motivation and commonsense systems that perusers can apply to their own lives. By examining the means these people took to analyze and recreate their propensity circles, we separate important examples on the mechanics of propensity change. The contextual analyses outline how unpretentious changes in signs, schedules, and rewards can prompt emotional enhancements in efficiency and in general prosperity.

This segment is a demonstration of the possibility that, no matter what the idea of our propensities or the difficulties we face, the standards of propensity circle change hold the way to opening our true capacity. Through these common encounters, perusers are urged to see their own propensities from a perspective of probability and to move toward the course of progress with reestablished positive thinking and lucidity.

Methodologies for Disturbing and Remaking Your Propensity Circles

Subsequent to uncovering the multifaceted subtleties of our propensity circles, the following essential step is figuring out how to disturb those that ruin our efficiency and prosperity, and how to build new, engaging ones in their stead. This part fills in as a manual for breaking liberated from the shackles of useless propensities and establishing the groundwork for schedules that push us towards our objectives.

Upsetting a propensity circle starts with changing its parts. By acquainting varieties with the signals, changing the daily schedule, or adjusting the normal award, we can debilitate the grasp of settled in propensities. This could mean updating our current circumstance to eliminate triggers for undesirable ways of behaving, or subbing a negative daily schedule with a more certain activity that satisfies a similar need. The pith of this system lies in imagination and trial and error, provoking ourselves to track down better approaches to accomplish the prizes we look for.

The reproduction of propensity circles is a conscious and smart cycle. It includes distinguishing the results we want and working in reverse to lay out schedules that lead to these prizes. This frequently requires a period of experimentation, as we investigate various prompts and rewards that rouse us to participate in the new daily schedule. Outcome in this try relies on tolerance, determination, and a readiness to adjust our methodologies as we realize what turns out best for us.

This segment gives a tool compartment to this extraordinary cycle, including techniques for outlining existing propensity circles, systems for conceptualizing elective schedules, and procedures for checking headway and adapting. Through connecting with accounts and contextual analyses, we represent the force of deliberate propensity adjustment, exhibiting people who have effectively reshaped their propensities to improve efficiency and fulfillment in their lives.

By embracing a purposeful way to deal with upsetting and remaking our propensity circles, we enable ourselves to assume command over our ways of behaving. This not just improves our capacity to accomplish our prompt objectives yet additionally makes way for long haul self-improvement and satisfaction. Outfitted with the techniques illustrated in this part, perusers are prepared to set out on an excursion of ceaseless personal development, utilizing the impact of trained instinct to open their maximum capacity.

3

Chapter 3: Keystone Habits: The Cornerstones of Success

Characterizing Cornerstone Propensities and Their Effect

In the tremendous scene of our ways of behaving, there exist specific propensities that hold the ability to emphatically change our lives. These are the cornerstone propensities, an idea that fills in as the foundation of this section. Not at all like standard schedules, cornerstone propensities have the one of a kind ability to begin a chain response, influencing different parts of our lives and prompting an outpouring of positive changes. These propensities work since they don't confine a solitary area of progress yet rather impact different ways of behaving and results at the same time.

Cornerstone propensities can be compared to the primary domino in a chain; once tipped, they lead to a progression of related changes that can significantly influence a singular's life. For instance, ordinary activity is much of the time refered to as a cornerstone propensity. It works on actual wellbeing as well as improves mental lucidity, supports mind-set, and increments energy levels, which thusly influence efficiency, connections, and individual discipline. The genuine force of cornerstone propensities lies in the immediate advantages they give as well as in their capacity to start a self-building up pattern of positive way of behaving and results.

This extraordinary effect is established in the manner cornerstone propensities make structures that advance other great practices. They assist with ingraining values and lay out schedules that become the structure inside which other positive propensities can thrive. Besides, cornerstone propensities frequently lead to the improvement of new abilities, the fortifying of individual character, and the support of confidence, laying a fruitful ground for long haul achievement and self-awareness.

Understanding cornerstone propensities and their significant effect is the most important move towards tackling this extraordinary power. As we dig further into this idea, we'll investigate the hypothesis behind cornerstone propensities as well as the down to earth parts of distinguishing and incorporating these propensities into our lives. By zeroing in on these significant schedules, we can open potential we never realized we had, showing ourselves a way to a more useful, satisfying, and effective life.

Distinguishing Your Cornerstone Propensities

At the center of groundbreaking change lie cornerstone propensities — those particular schedules with the ability to catalyze far reaching upgrades across different parts of our lives. The excursion to uncovering these crucial propensities starts with a profound plunge into the texture of our everyday schedules, looking for those exceptional exercises that can possibly set off a positive cascading type of influence. This part of the book is committed to directing you through the method involved with recognizing your own cornerstone propensities, those foundation rehearses that can open remarkable development and accomplishment.

The distinguishing proof of cornerstone propensities is both a craftsmanship and a science, requiring reflection, perception, and a touch of trial and error. These are the propensities that, once carried out, achieve a feeling of energy, empowering other good ways of behaving to stick to this same pattern. As far as some might be concerned, it very well may be a morning work-out schedule that ingrains a feeling of energy and reason over the course of the day. For other people, it very well may be the act of day to day arranging and reflection that brings clearness, concentration, and efficiency to their expert and individual lives.

To start this investigation, we welcome you to think about the parts of your life where you look for development and to consider the propensities that could act as impetuses for this change. Ask yourself which little activities appear to prompt other positive ways of behaving normally. Is it the demonstration of making your bed every morning that establishes the vibe for a day of request and achievement? Or on the other hand maybe it's the propensity for perusing for thirty minutes every night that spikes a more extensive obligation to constant learning and development.

This part offers a progression of activities intended to assist you with pinpointing your potential cornerstone propensities. Through directed reflection questions, conduct following, and examination of past triumphs, you'll be prepared to distinguish the schedules that have the ability to start inescapable change. Furthermore, we give models to assist you with recognizing straightforward everyday schedules and genuine cornerstone propensities, zeroing in on the effect, repeatability, and adaptability of these practices.

Distinguishing your cornerstone propensities is the most important phase in an excursion of change. It's tied in with finding those influence focuses in your standard that, when moved, have the ability to elevate and improve each and every part of your life. Through this cycle, you'll not just find the propensities that are critical to your self-improvement yet additionally figure out how to tackle their capability to make an existence of more prominent satisfaction and achievement.

Carrying out Cornerstone Propensities for Boundless Change

Having recognized the cornerstone propensities that hold the possibility to catalyze tremendous change in our lives, the following crucial step is to execute these propensities in a manner that guarantees their development and life span. This stage is tied in with transforming understanding right into it, implanting these strong schedules into the actual texture of our everyday presence. The excursion from acknowledgment to acknowledgment is both testing and fulfilling, requiring a mix of methodology, persistence, and strength.

The execution of cornerstone propensities starts with the rule of beginning little. About zeroing in on reasonable changes can be reliably applied. This approach assists with beating the inactivity of starting and the demoralization that can go with apparent difficulties. Whether it's devoting five minutes to reflection in the first part of the day or composing a solitary appreciation passage every evening, the accentuation is on laying out a standard that can be consistently based upon.

Consistency is the bedrock of this interaction. Cornerstone propensities get their power not from the size of the activity but rather from the consistency with which they're performed. This predictable application builds up the propensity circle, installing the new way of behaving into our brain connections, making it a characteristic and programmed piece of our daily schedule. Procedures to improve consistency could incorporate setting explicit prompts to set off the propensity, utilizing existing schedules as an establishment, or making responsibility through shared objectives.

Recognizing and anticipating the unavoidable difficulties is additionally vital. Obstruction can emerge out of inside, through fading inspiration, or from outside conditions that upset our schedules. To explore these snags, it's critical to keep an adaptable mentality, adjusting our methodologies depending on the situation while keeping our eyes on the overall objective. Procedures, for example, propensity stacking, where another propensity is attached to a current one, or the utilization of remunerations to support wanted ways of behaving, can be compelling devices in keeping up with energy.

This segment offers an extensive manual for inserting cornerstone propensities into your life, complete with noteworthy techniques, ways to conquer normal traps, and exhortation on utilizing the compound impacts of little changes. Through genuine models and master experiences, you'll learn how to start these extraordinary propensities as well as how to support them after some time, preparing for a fountain of positive changes across all parts of your life.

By purposely executing cornerstone propensities, we put into high gear a course of persistent improvement and self-disclosure. These propensities become the foundations of our prosperity, affecting our activities, however our personality, our attitude, and eventually, our fate.

Genuine Instances of Cornerstone Propensities in real life

The groundbreaking force of cornerstone propensities isn't simply hypothetical; it's distinctively delineated through the accounts of people and associations who have outfit these propensities to catalyze significant change. This part dives into an assortment of rousing genuine models, exhibiting the noteworthy effect that decisively picked and persistently applied cornerstone propensities can have on efficiency, prosperity, and in general achievement.

One such story is that of an independent company that moved its concentration towards cultivating a culture of persistent learning and improvement. By executing a cornerstone propensity for week by week group reflections and learning meetings, the organization saw an expanding influence that prompted superior cooperation, development, and representative fulfillment. This basic yet strong routine turned into the impetus for a more extensive hierarchical change, representing how a solitary cornerstone propensity can impact a whole corporate culture.

Another model comes from an individual battling with wellbeing and wellness. By recognizing early morning exercise as a cornerstone propensity, this individual better their actual wellbeing as well as experienced increased degrees of energy and concentration, prompting more useful days. The discipline and self-viability acquired from this propensity poured out over into their expert life, empowering them to handle difficulties with expanded versatility and inventiveness.

These accounts, among others highlighted in this segment, act as unmistakable proof of the cornerstone propensity idea in real life. They give a diagram to how distinguishing and supporting one critical propensity can prompt wide-arriving at changes, contacting each part of one's life. Through itemized investigation of these models, perusers gain experiences into the method involved with recognizing, executing, and profiting from their cornerstone propensities.

In addition, this segment stresses the comprehensiveness of cornerstone propensities, exhibiting that no matter what one's beginning stage, the conscious spotlight on developing critical schedules can prompt unprecedented results. It builds up the message that change is open to everybody, and that by zeroing in on key ways of behaving, people and associations the same can guide the course of their development and accomplishment.

The accounts shared here are not only accounts of progress; they are solicitations to activity. They allure perusers to consider their potential cornerstone propensities and to imagine the flowing impacts these propensities could release in their own lives. By interfacing the hypothetical underpinnings of cornerstone propensities with substantial instances of their power, this segment motivates perusers to leave on their excursion of change, furnished with the information that tremendous change is reachable, each propensity in turn.

4

Chapter 4: The Role of Belief in Habit Change

Grasping the Force of Conviction

At the center of each and every undertaking to improve on a propensity lies a crucial component more strong than any procedure or strategy: conviction. This part investigates the urgent job conviction plays in the domain of propensity change, laying out it as the foundation whereupon the structure of individual change is fabricated. Confidence in the chance of progress isn't simply helpful; it is fundamental. It powers the excursion from where we are to where we try to be, going about as both the flash that lights activity and the food that keeps the fire of progress consuming.

Conviction is the focal point through which we view our true capacity for change. It shapes our world, impacting how we decipher misfortunes and triumphs the same. When furnished with major areas of strength for an in our capacity to change, obstructions become conquerable, and disappointments are reclassified as venturing stones as opposed to endpoints. This groundbreaking force of conviction stretches out past simple hopefulness; a well established conviction can drive us to continue despite difficulty, to try different things with new methodologies, and to bounce back from the unavoidable difficulties that go with any endeavor at propensity change.

The excursion of modifying our propensities is loaded down with snapshots of uncertainty and allurement. It is at these times that conviction turns into our signal, directing us back to our way. It helps us to remember our purposes behind leaving on this excursion and revives our obligation to our objectives. The significance of developing a tough faith in the chance of progress couldn't possibly be more significant. Without it, the mechanics of propensity change — regardless of how deductively sound or skillfully applied — risk missing the mark concerning their true capacity.

This segment digs into the elements of conviction, outlining how it supports each step of the propensity change process. From the underlying choice to seek after another way to the everyday endeavors to implant new schedules, conviction is the string that interfaces our activities to our goals. The power changes the quest for change from a progression of mechanical activities into a significant excursion towards personal development.

By understanding the force of conviction, we outfit ourselves with a vital device for exploring the intricacies of propensity change. This section lays the basis for outfitting that power, making way for a more profound investigation of how we can develop and support confidence in our ability for change.

Conviction and the Cerebrum

The excursion of propensity change is profoundly entwined with the force of conviction, as a mental supporter as well as a power that can establish substantial, actual changes inside the actual cerebrum. This portion digs into the entrancing exchange among conviction and the cerebrum's pliancy, delineating what the conviction in our capacity to change means for our mentality as well as the actual wiring of our brain processes.

Neuroscience has divulged that our considerations and convictions can fundamentally influence the construction and capability of our cerebrums, a peculiarity known as brain adaptability. This pliancy is the cerebrum's capacity to rearrange itself by framing new brain associations over the course of life, permitting us to master new abilities, adjust to changes, and, critically, modify our propensities. At the point when we immovably have faith in our ability for transform, we're not simply wanting for an alternate result; we're effectively captivating our cerebrum in a course of independent overhauling.

Positive reasoning and perception assume key parts in this cycle. Imagining ourselves accomplishing an objective or dominating another propensity can enact the very brain networks that are engaged with the genuine exhibition of that way of behaving. This psychological practice takes action for change, making the ideal way of behaving simpler to embrace and the propensity bound to stick. Maybe our confidence in change sets the stage, and our mind answers by preparing for its part in the change.

Studies have shown that people who utilize positive representation methods and keep serious areas of strength for an in their capacity to change display more prominent brain movement in region of the cerebrum related with restraint and conduct guideline. These discoveries recommend that conviction doesn't simply rouse us to begin the excursion of propensity change; it truly prepares our cerebrum to actually explore this excursion more.

In this part, we investigate how to saddle the association among conviction and cerebrum versatility to work with propensity change. Through commonsense counsel and activities intended to reinforce conviction and positive perception, perusers will figure out how to connect with their cerebrum's versatility on the side of their propensity change endeavors. By getting it and applying the standards of conviction and the cerebrum, we open a strong partner in our journey to modify our propensities and reshape our lives.

Developing Conviction through Local area and Social Help

The way to enduring propensity change is only sometimes an excursion taken in isolation. As we explore the difficulties and wins of changing our propensities, the job of local area and social help arises as a critical power in developing and supporting our confidence in change.

This section investigates the significant effect of public bonds and shared yearnings on building up our conviction that change isn't just imaginable yet feasible.

Individuals are innately friendly animals, and our convictions, mentalities, and ways of behaving are significantly affected by individuals around us. At the point when we drench ourselves locally of people who share our objectives and values, we tap into an aggregate strength that can essentially reinforce our determination. Seeing others participate in the propensities we try to embrace or conquer the difficulties we face fills in as a strong update that our objectives are reachable. These social associations give motivation, yet an unmistakable feeling of responsibility that can drive us forward in any event, when our singular purpose might falter.

Besides, people group offer a rich embroidery of information, systems, and points of view that can improve how we might interpret propensity change. The common encounters and bits of knowledge of gathering individuals can enlighten the way forward, offering direction and backing that is both useful and profound. Whether it's through praising our victories or assisting us with exploring mishaps, the consolation and compassion of a strong local area can be a wellspring of inspiration.

This part digs into techniques for finding and drawing in with strong networks, whether they be online stages, neighborhood gatherings, or casual organizations of loved ones. It underlines the significance of choosing a local area that lines up with your qualities and objectives, and it offers direction on the best way to add to and get the most advantage from these social associations.

Through genuine models and significant guidance, perusers will figure out how to use the force of local area to reinforce their confidence in the chance of progress. By developing connections that confirm and uphold our yearnings, we upgrade our ability for self-improvement as well as add to a culture of aggregate strengthening. In the hug of a steady local area, the faith in change turns into a common conviction, changing the excursion of propensity change from a singular undertaking into an aggregate journey of disclosure and change.

Methodologies for Cultivating Faith in Change

Confidence in the chance of progress is definitely not a static quality that we either have or come up short on's; a unique express that can be developed and fortified after some time. This fundamental segment of the book gives a tool compartment of techniques intended to encourage a well established faith in private change, subsequently laying the basis for effective propensity change. Through viable strategies and careful practices, we can sustain an outlook that embraces change as well as effectively seeks after it as a pathway to self-awareness and satisfaction.

One essential system is the act of assertions. These positive, current state explanations are intended to check negative self-talk and build up our confidence in our capacity to change. By consistently recounting confirmations that emphasis on our assets, our true capacity, and our flexibility, we can move our inside discourse to one that upholds development and change.

Examples of overcoming adversity assume a significant part in cultivating conviction. Finding out about or perusing records of people who have effectively worked on their propensities can go about as strong inspirations. These accounts give substantial evidence that change is conceivable, offering knowledge into the methodologies that worked for other people and the deterrents they survived. By relating to these accounts, we can reinforce our own faith in our ability for change.

The idea of little wins is another indispensable methodology. Setting and accomplishing little, reasonable objectives can make a feeling of energy, constructing our certainty and building up our faith in our capacity to impact change. Every little success fills in as proof of our advancement, empowering us to handle bigger difficulties with expanded confidence.

At long last, it is central to define reachable objectives. Objectives that are too aggressive can be overpowering and may set us up for disappointment, sabotaging our confidence in change. By separating our bigger goals into more modest, significant stages, we make the course of progress more sensible and less overwhelming. This approach keeps us spurred as well as permits us to keep tabs on our development and praise our triumphs en route.

This part is improved with activities, reflections, and noteworthy hints that guide perusers through the most common way of building and keeping major areas of strength for an in their capacity to change. By utilizing these techniques, perusers will figure out how to develop a mentality that perspectives challenges as any open doors for development, difficulties as opportunities for growth, and change as a feasible reality. With a braced faith in change, perusers are prepared to set out on the excursion of propensity change with certainty and strength, prepared to open their maximum capacity and accomplish their most elevated goals.

5

Chapter 5: The Golden Rule of
Habit Change

Presenting the Brilliant Rule: Never Eliminate, Consistently Supplant
At the core of successful propensity change lies a straightforward yet
strong guideline: the Brilliant Rule of Propensity Change. This basic
decide states that to modify an unfortunate thing to do, one should not
endeavor to quench it however to substitute it with a more helpful way
of behaving. This section opens with a profound jump into the brain
science supporting this standard, revealing insight into why endeavors
to simply stop a propensity frequently make ready to backslide and disappointment.

The substance of the Brilliant Rule is established in the comprehension that propensities are more than simple activities; they are mind
boggling circles comprising of signs, schedules, and rewards. Attempting
to wipe out a propensity without tending to the basic need it satisfies
leaves a void that can prompt the resurgence of the old way of behaving
or the reception of another, possibly destructive, daily practice. Substitution, then again, regards the design of the propensity circle, offering a
manageable way to change by satisfying the first need in a better or more
useful way.

This way to deal with propensity change is grounded in the acknowledgment that our minds are wired for effectiveness. When a propensity circle is laid out, it turns into a default way for our viewpoints and activities. The Brilliant Rule use this brain wiring by embedding another daily practice into the current circle, subsequently keeping up with the productivity while changing the way of behaving. This strategy makes change more sensible as well as bound to stick, as it works with the mind's normal inclinations instead of against them.

Through connecting with stories and logical experiences, this part makes way for a groundbreaking excursion of propensity change. It provokes perusers to move their point of view from battling against undesirable propensities to imaginatively supplanting them. By embracing the Brilliant Rule, we furnish ourselves with a system that lines up with the complicated idea of human way of behaving and the cerebrum's components, setting a strong starting point for the parts that follow, which will direct perusers through the pragmatic utilization of this standard in their lives.

Applying the Brilliant Rule to Your Life

With the central comprehension of the Brilliant Rule — never eliminate a propensity, consistently supplant it — this segment changes into pragmatic application, offering an outline for incorporating this guideline into the texture of your day to day existence. Here, we explore the nuanced interaction of changing comprehension right into it, directing you through the means important to saddle the impact of trained instinct substitution across assorted parts of your life, from wellbeing and efficiency to individual prosperity.

The most important phase in this groundbreaking excursion is the distinguishing proof of the propensity to be changed. This requires a time of reflection and perception, where you index your schedules and the signals and rewards related with them. Understanding the job each propensity plays in your day to day existence enlightens the way to tracking down a reasonable substitution that tends to similar necessities without the unfortunate results.

When an objective propensity is recognized, the quest for a

substitution starts. This critical stage includes conceptualizing potential new propensities that satisfy similar prizes as the old ones yet adjust all the more intimately with your qualities and objectives. The determination interaction is profoundly private and requires thought of your special inclinations, way of life, and the items of common sense of your day to day daily schedule. The point is to find a substitution propensity that not just fills a similar need as the old propensity yet additionally feels fulfilling and supportable by its own doing.

Executing the new propensity includes arranging and planning. This could incorporate modifying your current circumstance to help the new everyday practice, getting ready apparatuses or assets expected to play out the new propensity, and booking explicit times to take part in the way of behaving. Consistency is critical; the new propensity ought to be polished consistently in light of the very signal that set off the old propensity, guaranteeing a smooth change in your brain connections from the old daily schedule to the new.

To harden the new propensity, support procedures like following advancement, commending achievements, and utilizing social help can be inconceivably viable. These practices not just upgrade the prize of the new propensity yet in addition strengthen your obligation to the change, making the new standard an essential piece of your personality and day to day existence.

This segment is loaded with significant counsel, procedures, and tips intended to enable you to successfully apply the Brilliant Rule. Through definite direction and steady bits of knowledge, you are prepared to explore the excursion of propensity supplanting with certainty, changing your desires for change into substantial real factors.

Methods for Tracking down Successful Substitutions

Recognizing a viable trade for an undesired propensity is both a craftsmanship and a science, requiring a profound comprehension of one's necessities, ways of behaving, and the triggers that start propensity circles. This essential stage in the propensity change process includes a careful assessment of the signs and rewards driving the old propensity, determined to track down another propensity that fulfills similar requirements in a better or more useful way. This part dives into the procedures and contemplations fundamental for choosing substitution propensities that are compelling as well as supportable and satisfying.

The most important phase in finding a successful substitution is to take apart the first propensity, understanding the fundamental need it satisfies. Is it stress help, a feeling of remuneration, or maybe a method for mingling? By pinpointing the center capability of the propensity, you can start to conceptualize elective activities that meet similar need without the adverse results. This includes inventive reasoning and a readiness to explore different avenues regarding various exercises until you find one that reverberates.

Similarly significant is the similarity of the new propensity with your way of life and inclinations. A fruitful substitution propensity should not just location a similar need as the old propensity yet do as such in a manner that is open and pleasant for you. For example, in the event that the objective is to supplant a stationary night schedule with something more dynamic, the option ought to be an action that you truly appreciate and can reasonably integrate into your everyday existence, whether it's a dance class, a daily walk, or a yoga meeting at home.

Trial and error assumes a basic part in this cycle. It's improbable that the main substitution propensity you attempt will be the ideal fit. Be ready to evaluate a few distinct exercises, giving close consideration to how well they fulfill the first sign and prize, and that keeping up with them over the long haul is so doable. This experimentation approach isn't just ordinary yet vital for finding the best fit for your extraordinary conditions.

At last, assessing the appropriateness of potential substitutions includes observing your reaction to the new propensity. Does it really fulfill the signal and give a practically identical or preferable compensation over the old propensity? Is it safe to say that you are ready to keep up with consistency? The solutions to these inquiries are significant marks of the adequacy of the substitution propensity.

This segment furnishes perusers with an extensive tool stash for exploring the intricacies of propensity substitution, offering functional activities, intelligent inquiries, and techniques for experimentation. By applying these methods, you are exceptional to recognize substitution propensities that disturb undesirable schedules as well as improve your general personal satisfaction, preparing for enduring change.

Examples of overcoming adversity of Applying the Brilliant Rule

The groundbreaking force of supplanting instead of killing propensities turns out to be most unmistakable through the tales of the individuals who have experienced this change. This segment uncovers moving genuine instances of people who have effectively applied the Brilliant Rule of Propensity Change, offering both inspiration and down to earth bits of knowledge for perusers setting out on their own excursion of change.

One such story is that of Maria, a product designer who wound up trapped in a pattern of late-evening nibbling while at the same time dealing with her tasks. This propensity impacted her wellbeing as well as her efficiency and rest quality. By applying the Brilliant Rule, Maria supplanted her evening time nibbling with a short contemplation meeting, tending to her requirement for a break and stress help without falling back on food. This basic however successful change worked on her actual wellbeing as well as her concentration and effectiveness in her work.

Another model comes from Alex, an undergrad battling with hesitation, frequently occupied by virtual entertainment. Perceiving that his propensity originated from a requirement for social association and intermittent breaks from contemplating, Alex supplanted his virtual entertainment use with booked espresso gatherings with companions and short, coordinated breaks during concentrate on meetings. This substitution met his hidden necessities as well as improved his scholarly execution and public activity, exhibiting the complex advantages of powerful propensity substitution.

These accounts, and others highlighted in this part, feature the assorted ways the Brilliant Rule can be executed across various everyday issues. From further developing wellbeing and efficiency to upgrading individual connections and prosperity, the guideline of propensity substitution ends up being an amazing asset for accomplishing objectives and cultivating self-awareness.

Through nitty gritty investigations of these examples of overcoming adversity, perusers gain important bits of knowledge into the method involved with recognizing, carrying out, and supporting substitution propensities. The difficulties experienced and the procedures utilized by these people give pragmatic examples and support to anybody hoping to roll out certain improvements in their day to day existence.

This segment serves as a wellspring of motivation as well as a demonstration of the viability of the Brilliant Rule in working with enduring propensity change. By sharing these stories, we expect to engage perusers with the certainty that change is conceivable and that by decisively supplanting propensities, they can fundamentally work on their lives and accomplish their most noteworthy yearnings.

6

Chapter 6: The Habit of Productivity

Characterizing Efficiency With regards to Propensity

In the excursion toward individual and expert satisfaction, efficiency arises not only as a measurement of what we achieve yet as a foundation propensity that supports our regular routines. This part rethinks efficiency, lifting it from a progression of result driven undertakings to a profoundly instilled propensity that shapes our way to deal with work, imagination, and self-improvement. By review efficiency from the perspective of ongoing way of behaving, we progress from irregular eruptions of proficiency to a supported culture of viability that is woven into the texture of our ordinary presence.

Efficiency, in its quintessence, is the propensity for making deliberate and intentional utilization within recent memory, energy, and assets. It includes a change in context — from seeking after hecticness to accomplishing significant advancement in our undertakings. This calculated shift is critical; it perceives that genuine efficiency isn't tied in with filling each second with movement however about guaranteeing that our activities line up with our most esteemed objectives and yearnings.

At the core of useful conduct lies a progression of miniature propensities — little, repeatable activities that by and large cow us towards our targets. These miniature propensities could incorporate the manners in which we focus on undertakings, how we oversee interruptions, or the strategies we utilize to keep up with concentration and inspiration over the course of the day. Every one of these ways of behaving, when rehashed reliably, adds to the improvement of an efficiency propensity that is both strong and versatile.

The change of efficiency into a propensity requests something other than discipline; it requires a profound comprehension of our own rhythms and work styles. It provokes us to be aware of how we apportion our time, to define limits that safeguard our energy, and to refine our cycles in quest for greatness persistently. By inserting efficiency into our constant schedules, we make a structure for living that upholds the accomplishment of our nearby errands as well as the acknowledgment of our drawn out dreams.

This segment lays the foundation for reconsidering efficiency as a propensity, offering another worldview for understanding how we can develop a way of life that champions proficiency, inventiveness, and satisfaction. From this perspective, efficiency turns out to be something other than an objective to try to — it turns into an approach to being, a center propensity that moves us towards our most elevated potential.

Recognizing Efficiency Propensities and Their Triggers

Leaving on the way to upgraded efficiency starts with a cautious assessment of our ongoing propensities and the triggers that start them. This essential step includes digging into the schedules that comprise our days, knowing which practices impel us toward productivity and which diminish our adequacy. By distinguishing the propensities at the core of our efficiency — or scarcity in that department — we open the capacity to create a more deliberate and productive day to day beat.

The triggers of useful propensities frequently lie in the unpretentious signals dissipated all through our current circumstance and timetable. These can go from the actual design of our work area, which can either empower centered work or lead to interruptions, to the hour of day when we feel generally stimulated and equipped for handling testing undertakings. Close to home states likewise assume a vital part; sensations of inspiration or uneasiness can act as signs that quick us to participate in useful or counterproductive ways of behaving.

Understanding these triggers requires a mix of contemplation and perception. Keeping a propensity diary, for example, can enlighten designs in our way of behaving, uncovering the circumstances under which we are probably going to be useful. This mindfulness permits us to control our current circumstance and timetable to duplicate these circumstances, subsequently improving the probability of participating in useful propensities.

This section guides perusers through the most common way of recognizing their own efficiency propensities and the triggers that start them. It stresses the significance of being aware of both the positive schedules that drive progress and the negative examples that block it. Through down to earth practices and intelligent inquiries, perusers are urged to delineate their efficiency propensities, acquiring knowledge into the signs that expeditious these ways of behaving and the prizes they look to get.

By demystifying the triggers behind our efficiency propensities, we outfit ourselves with the information to establish a climate that encourages concentration, proficiency, and fulfillment. This understanding upgrades our capacity to be useful as well as engages us to assume command over our day to day routines, molding our schedules in a way that lines up with our objectives and values. Through this cycle, efficiency rises above the domain of undertakings and tasks, turning into a propensity that improves our expert and individual undertakings.

Making a Day to day Propensity Outline for Efficiency

To tackle the propensity for efficiency, one should set out on a smart course of planning a day to day diagram — an organized at this point adaptable arrangement that frames how to explore the day with expectation and proficiency. This outline isn't just a timetable or a plan for the day; an essential structure coordinates efficiency propensities into the beat of regular daily existence, guaranteeing that each activity lines up with one's more extensive objectives and values.

The formation of this plan starts with lucidity on how efficiency affects you. It requires distinguishing the results that make the biggest difference, whether they're connected with professional success, self-improvement, wellbeing, or connections. From this groundwork of understanding, you can begin to develop a day to day schedule that focuses on these region, guaranteeing that your most significant undertakings get the consideration and energy they merit.

A basic part of the day to day propensity outline is the acknowledgment and the executives of time. This includes not simply the distribution of hours and minutes to explicit assignments however understanding when during the day you are generally ready, innovative, and viable. By adjusting your most difficult or significant work with these pinnacle periods, you streamline your efficiency and guarantee that your endeavors yield the best effect.

Similarly significant is the joining of breaks and awards into your day to day plan. Efficiency isn't about constant work; it's about practical advancement. Planned stops, whether for a short walk, reflection, or a side interest, act as fundamental resets that forestall burnout and keep up with elevated degrees of commitment and innovativeness. Rewards, whether they're straightforward joys or bigger motivating forces, build up the positive propensity circle of efficiency, causing it more probable that you'll to stick to your plan reliably.

This part of the book furnishes perusers with the apparatuses and systems to create their customized everyday propensity plan. It offers direction on laying out boundaries, overseeing time, adjusting energy, and consolidating breaks and prizes in a way that supports supported efficiency. Through formats, activities, and models, perusers are prepared to make a day to day system that improves their effectiveness as well as adds to their general prosperity and satisfaction.

By embracing an everyday propensity outline for efficiency, you make a critical stride towards changing your desires into accomplishments. This organized way to deal with every day engages you to explore your errands with concentration and reason, transforming the propensity for efficiency into a foundation of your way of life.

Instruments and Applications That Can Help Construct and Track Efficiency Propensities

During a time where innovation is unpredictably woven into the texture of our day to day routines, utilizing computerized instruments and applications can fundamentally improve our capacity to fabricate and keep up with efficiency propensities. This part dives into an organized choice of instruments and applications intended to help propensity development, task the board, and efficiency following. By giving an outline of these advanced guides, we plan to furnish you with assets that work with the development of useful propensities as well as proposition bits of knowledge into your examples of work and rest, empowering you to refine your methodology over the long haul.

Task the board applications act as the foundation of efficiency, permitting you to sort out your errands, put forth boundaries, and timetable cutoff times. These devices frequently include abilities for arranging assignments into ventures or areas of concentration, empowering you to envision the master plan while dealing with the subtleties. By separating your targets into significant stages, these applications help to demystify the way toward your objectives, gaining ground substantial and quantifiable.

Propensity following applications offer an everyday log of your ways of behaving, giving a visual portrayal of your consistency and regions for development. The demonstration of recording your propensities can build up your obligation to them, transforming conceptual desires into substantial activities. A significant number of these applications likewise consolidate highlights, for example, updates and persuasive statements, filling in as both a poke and a wellspring of motivation to keep you lined up with your efficiency objectives.

Pomodoro clocks and center apparatuses are intended to upgrade focus and oversee interruptions. By dividing work into centered stretches, normally 25 minutes, trailed by brief breaks, these instruments assist with developing a beat of supported consideration and rest. This method supports productivity as well as mitigates weariness, making your work meetings more compelling.

At last, care and prosperity applications add to efficiency by tending to its primary angle: mental and actual wellbeing. These applications offer assets for reflection, stress the board, and rest improvement, perceiving that a refreshed psyche and a solid body are requirements for supported efficiency. By integrating these practices into your day to day daily schedule, you support your general ability to center, make, and accomplish.

This part presents a scope of computerized instruments as well as offers direction on the most proficient method to coordinate them successfully into your everyday propensity outline. Through customized proposals and commonsense tips, you'll figure out how to choose and use these applications to help your remarkable work process, improving your capacity to keep up with center, oversee time, and at last, develop a propensity for efficiency that supports your prosperity.

7

Chapter 7: Overcoming Obstacles to Habit Change

Normal Difficulties in Making progress with Propensities

Leaving on the excursion of propensity change is similar to heading out on unfamiliar waters. It requires an unmistakable objective as well as the strength to explore through unavoidable difficulties. This segment digs into the normal hindrances that one could experience chasing changing propensities. Perceiving and understanding these difficulties is the most important move toward defeating them.

Protection from change is many times the primary boundary. This obstruction can originate from different sources — solace in commonality, anxiety toward disappointment, or the overwhelming possibility of getting out of one's usual range of familiarity. Propensities, by their actual nature, are imbued examples of conduct that give a feeling of consistency and security. Modifying these examples requests a takeoff from the known, wandering into a space where results are dubious.

One more pervasive test is the misstatement of the time and exertion expected to impart new propensities. Many leave on the excursion of propensity change with assumptions for speedy outcomes, just to find that significant change requires diligent exertion over the long haul. This error among assumption and reality can prompt dissatisfaction and de-motivation, impeding advancement.

Outer variables, like natural signals and prevailing difficulties, additionally assume a huge part in forming our propensities. The climate we possess is weighed down with triggers that can prompt programmed ways of behaving, frequently without our cognizant mindfulness. Also, the impact of groups of friends can build up existing propensities, making change seriously testing without any help or understanding from everyone around us.

Finally, slips in self-restraint and inspiration are normal hindrances. The excursion of propensity change isn't straight; it includes ups and downs, triumphs and difficulties. During times of low inspiration or when confronted with enticements, the discipline to finish what has been started can disappear, prompting slips in the reception of new propensities.

This part features these difficulties as well as makes way for investigating techniques to actually explore them. By recognizing the hindrances that lie ahead, we arm ourselves with the information and readiness expected to deal with them directly, transforming difficulties into venturing stones on the way to effective propensity change.

Techniques for Defeating Opposition and Losing the faith

In the journey for propensity change, experiencing opposition and encountering losing the faith are not indications of disappointment but rather normal components of the human experience. This part of the book offers an encouraging sign and down to earth techniques for the people who wind up grappling with these difficulties, giving a guide to exploring through the difficult situations of progress.

Most importantly, the force of little, steady advances couldn't possibly be more significant. The excursion of 1,000 miles starts with a solitary step, and the way to propensity change is the same. By separating the overall objective into more modest, sensible assignments, the cycle turns out to be less overwhelming, diminishing obstruction and making the possibility of progress more congenial. This approach not just works with simpler incorporation of new propensities into day to day existence yet additionally gives a progression of feasible achievements that can support inspiration and certainty.

Care and mindfulness are basic apparatuses in fighting opposition. By developing a mindful and non-critical consciousness of our viewpoints and activities, we can distinguish the triggers of opposition and comprehend the feelings and convictions powering it. This mindfulness permits us to answer these triggers with aim instead of respond consequently, making a space where decision and change are conceivable.

Establishing a strong climate is another key methodology. This includes both changing your actual environmental elements to decrease enticements and signs related with the old propensity and looking for or establishing a strong social climate. Encircling yourself with individuals who support your objectives and comprehend the difficulties you're confronting can give consolation and responsibility, fundamental components for keeping up with inspiration through the high points and low points of propensity change.

At long last, fostering an alternate course of action for managing mishaps and breaking faith is fundamental. Change is a unique interaction, and mishaps are an inescapable piece of the excursion. As opposed to survey them as disappointments, consider them to be chances to learn and develop. An alternate course of action that incorporates predefined systems for refocusing after a difficulty can have the effect between a brief slip and a total backslide.

This part offers not just understanding into the idea of obstruction and losing the faith yet additionally significant guidance for beating these impediments. Through reasonable activities, intelligent inquiries, and genuine models, perusers will figure out how to expect difficulties, foster successful survival techniques, and construct flexibility, guaranteeing that they stay immovable on their way to enduring propensity change.

The Job of Climate in Supporting or Impeding Propensity Change

The spaces where we reside and work hold a significant impact over our propensities, frequently in manners we could not completely appreciate. This segment investigates how our current circumstance can either act as a bedrock for positive propensity change or, on the other hand, go about as a boundary to our advancement. Perceiving and decisively adjusting our environmental factors can emphatically expand our opportunities to effectively embrace new propensities and eliminating unwanted ones.

A steady climate is one that limits grinding towards taking part in certain propensities and increments grating for negative ones. Straightforward changes, like keeping sound tidbits inside simple reach or putting running shoes close to the bed, can make participating in certain propensities more easy. On the other hand, by adding boundaries to negative propensities —, for example, moving snacks to a high rack or leaving Mastercards at home to keep away from drive buys — we can fundamentally lessen their event.

Past the actual arrangement, the social climate assumes an essential part. Individuals with whom we invest our energy can impact our conduct through accepted practices, assumptions, and backing. Encircling ourselves with people who epitomize the propensities we seek to can rouse us and give a living outline to how those propensities can be coordinated into our own lives. Besides, communicating our objectives to our group of friends can enroll their help and consider us responsible, making it harder to lose the faith without notice.

In any case, not all natural variables are inside our control, and it is critical to perceive this. Working environments, family responsibilities, and cultural standards can make imperatives that make propensity change testing. In these cases, zeroing in on what can be controlled and tracking down imaginative ways of adjusting to or relieve the impact of less pliable parts of our current circumstance are key systems.

This segment furnishes perusers with functional systems for surveying and reshaping their surroundings to help their propensity change objectives. Through a progression of activities and agendas, perusers will figure out how to direct a natural review of their own and proficient spaces, recognize changes that can uphold their new propensities, and execute procedures to manage the pieces of their current circumstance that are unchangeable as far as they might be concerned.

Toward the finish of this part, perusers will have acquired a complete comprehension of the basic job climate plays in propensity change and will be furnished with the devices to make their environmental factors a strong partner in their excursion towards individual change.

The most effective method to Establish a Favorable Climate for Change

Creating a climate that encourages propensity change is similar to setting up the dirt for planting: it requires insightful arrangement, sustaining, and the right circumstances to help development. This segment is a manual for establishing such a climate, one that upholds the reception of new propensities as well as supports them over the long haul. Through conscious plan and deliberate decisions, you can change your environmental elements into an impetus for individual development and achievement.

The most important phase in establishing a favorable climate for change is to wipe out interruptions and enticements that lead to unwanted propensities. This could mean cleaning up your work area to encourage concentration or utilizing applications that limit your admittance to diverting sites. By eliminating these deterrents, you clear a smoother way toward taking part in additional useful ways of behaving.

Then, incorporate obvious signals and tokens of your objectives into your current circumstance. Putting persuasive statements, objective outlines, or even visual portrayals of your advancement in essential areas can act as steady tokens of your responsibilities and goals. These visual prompts keep your objectives top of brain as well as support your inspiration and concentration.

Another system is to use innovation and apparatuses intended to work with propensity change. Whether it's utilizing propensity following applications to screen your advancement, booking programming to design your days, or computerized stages that associate you with a steady local area, innovation can be a strong partner in making a construction that energizes and upholds your development.

At last, it is vital to encourage a steady friendly climate. This includes searching out or making a local area of similar people who are likewise dedicated to self-awareness and propensity change. Imparting your excursion to others gives a feeling of fellowship and responsibility, making the cycle not so much detaching but rather more improving. Whether through web-based discussions, nearby gatherings, or even inside your circles and family, fabricating an organization of help can essentially upgrade your capacity to remain focused on your new propensities.

This segment offers an extensive way to deal with reshaping your physical, computerized, and social conditions in manners that help your propensity change objectives. Through functional counsel, genuine models, and significant stages, perusers will figure out how to build an encompassing that obliges change as well as effectively advances it. Toward the finish of this part, you will have the information and devices to make a space that supports your desires, diverting the climate from a possible hindrance into a strong facilitator of individual change.

8

Chapter 8: Habit Stacking and Compound Growth

The Idea of Propensity Stacking

At the core of changing our day to day schedules lies a strong, yet surprisingly straightforward technique known as propensity stacking. This imaginative way to deal with propensity arrangement permits us to mesh new propensities into the texture of our current schedules by mooring them to ways of behaving we as of now perform consequently. By connecting new propensities to laid out ones, we make a chain of activities that stream normally starting with one then onto the next, decreasing the psychological exertion expected to take on new ways of behaving and fundamentally upgrading our capacity to keep up with them over the long haul.

Propensity stacking is predicated on the rule that each propensity is moored by a signal that triggers it, trailed by the everyday practice of the actual propensity, and finishing in a prize. At the point when we "stack" another propensity onto a current one, we utilize the current propensity's prompt and award as the extension for integrating the new way of behaving. For example, in the event that you as of now have a propensity for blending some espresso every morning, you could stack the propensity for pondering for five minutes following turning on the espresso machine. Along these lines, the laid out propensity not just reminds you to participate in the new propensity yet in addition gives a construction that causes the expansion to feel like a characteristic expansion of your morning schedule.

The excellence of propensity stacking lies in its effortlessness and adaptability. It tends to be applied to essentially any everyday issue, from wellbeing and wellness to efficiency, individual budget, and then some. Whether you're hoping to integrate greater development into your day, work on your abilities in a specific region, or cultivate better wellbeing rehearses, propensity stacking offers a clear way to advance.

This segment of the book acquaints perusers with the fundamental ideas of propensity stacking, investigating the mental science that supports it and giving a reasonable system to utilizing this procedure in their own lives. Through drawing in clarifications and illustrative models, you will find how to recognize likely stacks in your day to day daily practice and start the most common way of building a more extravagant, more useful example of propensities. By excelling at propensity stacking, you open a useful asset for self-improvement, one that tackles the energy of your current propensities to move you toward your objectives effortlessly and proficiency.

Step by step instructions to Actually Stack Propensities for Compound Development

To bridle the groundbreaking trained instinct stacking, one should explore the interaction with both expectation and methodology. This part fills in as a reasonable manual for building successful propensity stacks that encourage the reception of new ways of behaving as well as compound their advantages over the long run, prompting dramatic self-awareness.

The groundwork of compelling propensity stacking is the cautious determination and sequencing of propensities. The key is to begin with a deep rooted propensity, one that is so imbued in your everyday schedule that it requires no thought. This propensity fills in as the anchor for your stack. From that point, the new propensity you decide to add ought to be consistently associated with the anchor propensity, guaranteeing a smooth change starting with one activity then onto the next. For instance, on the off chance that your anchor propensity is cleaning your teeth each day, you could stack a propensity for confirming your day to day objectives just in the wake of, utilizing the energy of your laid out everyday practice to support your concentration for the afternoon.

Straightforwardness and particularity are critical in picking which propensities to stack. The new propensity ought to be already straightforward to perform without critical exertion following the anchor propensity. It ought to likewise be explicit, with an unmistakable activity that rules out uncertainty. This explicitness helps in shaping an exact prompt for the new propensity, making it simpler to recall and execute.

Keeping up with energy in propensity stacking is fundamental. To do this, emphasis on each stack in turn. Attempting to present various stacks at the same time can weaken your concentration and sabotage your endeavors. When a stack has been effectively coordinated into your daily schedule — becoming as programmed as the first propensity — you can consider adding one more layer to your stack or making another stack somewhere else in your everyday practice.

Moreover, it's critical to be patient and consider adaptability. A few stacks may not fill in as expected, requiring changes or replacements of propensities. This iterative interaction is an ordinary piece of tracking down the best fit for your extraordinary way of life and objectives.

This segment furnishes perusers with an organized way to deal with planning and executing their propensity stacks, complete with ways to choose the right propensities, sequencing them for most extreme effect, and investigating normal issues. Through itemized models and noteworthy counsel, you'll figure out how to use propensity stacking as a strong component for driving compound development, empowering you to construct a more extravagant, seriously satisfying life each propensity in turn.

Instances of Fruitful Propensity Stacking

The hypothesis of propensity stacking changes into a striking story through the tales of the individuals who have woven this technique into the embroidery of their lives, accomplishing noteworthy changes. This segment focuses on an assortment of motivating models, exhibiting the different and strong manners by which people have bridled the impact of trained instinct stacking to catalyze critical self-improvement and improvement.

One story acquaints us with Emma, an independent visual planner who battled with keeping a reliable work-out daily schedule. By stacking a fifteen-minute yoga pursue onto her morning routine of fermenting espresso, Emma tracked down an approach to flawlessly incorporate wellness into her everyday existence. The demonstration of hanging tight for her espresso turned into the signal to unroll her yoga mat, prompting an extended time of continuous everyday practice that upgraded her actual prosperity and mental clearness.

Another story highlights Alex, a bustling programmer planning to further develop his language abilities in the midst of a requesting work plan. Alex chose to stack language learning onto his night schedule of getting ready supper. By paying attention to language learning web recordings while cooking, he used a generally casual exercise as a chance for development. This basic expansion made his way of learning easy as well as changed his eating times into a useful and charming piece of his day.

Through these models and that's just the beginning, this part delineates the versatility of propensity stacking across different spaces of life, from wellbeing and wellness to learning and efficiency. Every story not just subtleties the propensities associated with the stack yet additionally features the difficulties confronted, techniques utilized, and the effect of these progressions on the people's lives.

Perusers will track down in these stories a wellspring of motivation and a diagram for applying propensity stacking to their own lives. Whether it's upgrading individual prosperity, getting new abilities, or further developing efficiency, the models show that with imagination and perseverance, propensity stacking can open ways to additional opportunities and pathways to accomplishment.

By displaying genuine utilizations of propensity stacking, this segment plans to enlighten the unmistakable advantages of this methodology, giving perusers the certainty and inspiration to explore different avenues regarding their propensity stacks and witness the compound development that unfurls.

Making arrangements for Long haul Accomplishment Through Steady Changes

The excursion of propensity stacking isn't a run however a long distance race, a progression of steady changes that, over the long run, lead to significant change and compound development. This part is committed to directing perusers through the most common way of making arrangements for long haul achievement, underscoring the significance of tolerance, perseverance, and versatility in supporting a way of life that constantly develops towards more noteworthy satisfaction and accomplishment.

The foundation of long haul outcome in propensity stacking is the acknowledgment of the total force of little changes. Like the accumulating revenue of a bank account, every little propensity added to your day to day schedule expands upon the last, dramatically expanding your development after some time. This point of view empowers an emphasis on consistency instead of power, featuring the benefit of making reasonable, sensible increments to your life.

Vital arranging assumes a pivotal part in this cycle. Setting clear, long haul objectives gives guidance, while stalling objectives down into noteworthy advances offers a guide for slow improvement. Each propensity stack you make ought to line up with these more extensive goals, guaranteeing that each steady change carries you nearer to your definitive vision.

Flexibility is likewise key. As you progress, your necessities, conditions, and objectives might move, expecting changes in accordance with your propensity stacks. Consistently surveying and refining your schedules guarantees that they stay important and successful. This iterative methodology permits you to remain receptive to life's changes, transforming snags into open doors for additional development.

At long last, praising achievements and considering your process cultivates a pride and appreciation that energizes your inspiration. Perceiving the distance you've voyaged, regarding your propensities as well as in your self-improvement, builds up the effect of your endeavors and the benefit of forging ahead with this way.

This part offers a diagram for inserting propensity stacking into the texture of your life, with reasonable exhortation on arranging, execution, and transformation. Through illustrative models, perusers will perceive the way steady changes, directed by smart preparation and advanced by reflection, can prompt huge compound development. By embracing the standards illustrated here, you can establish the groundwork for a daily existence portrayed by nonstop improvement, making way for enduring achievement and satisfaction.

Conclusion

Recap of Central issues and Techniques

As we end this excursion through the complexities of propensity arrangement and change, it's fundamental for stop and think about the ground we've covered. All along, this book has been a compass pointed toward directing you through the scene of individual change, with a definitive objective of excelling at efficiency through the impact of trained instinct.

We started by disentangling the life systems of propensities, presenting the propensity circle as the foundation of propensity development. Figuring out the signals, schedules, and rewards that drive our ways of behaving enlightened the way to changing or supplanting propensities that never again serve us. This establishment set up for more profound investigation into the components of progress, from the distinguishing proof and influence of cornerstone propensities that start fountains of positive change, to the basic job of confidence in beating the idleness of old examples.

The excursion likewise took us through the essential course of propensity stacking, where new propensities are piggybacked onto laid out ones, making a platform for development that coordinates flawlessly into our regular routines. We dug into the meaning of establishing a favorable climate for change, perceiving that our environmental elements can either uphold or sabotage our endeavors at propensity change.

En route, we were acquainted with useful apparatuses and methods intended to make the course of progress more reasonable and powerful. From utilizing innovation to help propensity following and efficiency, to taking on care rehearses that upgrade our mindfulness and command over our activities, the systems framed in this book are expected to act as a tool compartment for anybody hoping to tackle the groundbreaking force of propensities.

This restates the central issues and methodologies examined as well as fills in as a sign of the excursion's worth. The bits of knowledge acquired and the instruments procured are venturing stones on the way to a more useful, satisfied, and reason driven life.

The Nonstop Excursion of Propensity Improvement and Authority

As we finish up this investigation of propensities and their extraordinary potential, it's essential to recognize that the excursion toward propensity improvement and dominance is certainly not a limited one. All things being equal, it unfurls ceaselessly, advancing as we do, across the scene of our lives. This quest for self-awareness through propensity change is a continuous cycle, checked not by a last objective but rather by the achievements we accomplish and the illustrations we advance en route.

The pith of this excursion lies in its dynamism and the unending open door it offers for self-disclosure and reexamination. Each propensity we try to change, each new conduct we mean to embrace, carries us nearer to understanding our actual potential and the horde ways we can form our lives to mirror our most elevated desires. It is a way cleared with victories and mishaps the same, each conveying priceless bits of knowledge into our versatility, our ability for change, and the unlimited conceivable outcomes that exist in the domain of routine activity.

Embracing the consistent idea of this excursion requires a mentality secured in persistence, determination, and a readiness to confront the difficulties that emerge with a feeling of interest and transparency. It requires a guarantee to flexibility, perceiving that as our conditions, objectives, and selves change, so too should our propensities. This liquid way to deal with self-awareness guarantees that our excursion of propensity improvement stays significant, responsive, and lavishly fulfilling.

In this never-ending pattern of learning and development, the dominance of propensities arises not as a static accomplishment but rather as a consistently advancing practice. A discipline welcomes us to stay long lasting students, continually investigating new techniques, refining our methodologies, and developing comprehension we might interpret the unpredictable dance between our activities and our results.

As we push ahead, let us convey with us the examples gathered from this investigation, clutching the information that the excursion of propensity improvement is perhaps of the most significant venture we can make in ourselves. It is a demonstration of our innate limit with regards to change and a recognition for the unstoppable human soul's journey for greatness, satisfaction, and an existence of intentional activity.

Consolation to Examination and Find What Works Best

As we explore the complex and profoundly private excursion of propensity change, one of the most engaging acknowledge is that there is nobody size-fits-all arrangement. The scene of our lives, with its remarkable difficulties, objectives, and rhythms, requests a fitted way to deal with propensity development and change. This part fills in as a support to embrace the soul of trial and error, to move toward the craft of propensity change with interest, and to find through experimentation the methodologies that reverberate most significantly with you.

Setting out on this exploratory excursion requires a receptive outlook and a readiness to wander past the solace of natural schedules. It welcomes you to blend and match procedures talked about all through this book, to join them in creative ways, and to change them as per your advancing necessities and conditions. The method involved with finding what turns out best for you isn't just about accomplishing your ideal results; it's tied in with studying yourself, your inspirations, your protections, and your abilities for change.

Trial and error likewise includes embracing disappointment not as a misfortune but rather as a fundamental piece of the growing experience. Each endeavor, regardless of whether effective, gives important experiences that can refine your methodology and carry you nearer to the propensities that will genuinely improve your life. This mentality changes the excursion of propensity change from an overwhelming errand into an interesting investigation, brimming with open doors for development and disclosure.

To work with this investigation, think about keeping a propensity diary where you can record your tests, consider their results, and change your techniques likewise. This training helps in keeping tabs on your development as well as in distinguishing examples and experiences that can direct your future endeavors.

In empowering you to trial and find what works best, this segment helps you that the excursion to remember propensity change is profoundly private and limitlessly variable. It support the possibility that through steadiness, inventiveness, and self-reflection, you can create a bunch of propensities that are powerful as well as remarkably yours, mirroring your singular way to satisfaction and achievement.

Last Contemplations on the Groundbreaking Force of Propensities

As we finish up our investigation of the specialty of propensity arrangement and change, it's fundamental to think about the significant effect that dominating our propensities can have on our lives. The excursion we've set out upon isn't only about changing our day to day schedules however about opening our true capacity for significant individual change. Through the essential forming of our propensities, we have the ability to improve our efficiency, accomplish our most aggressive objectives, and develop an existence of profound fulfillment and reason.

The standards and systems illustrated in this book highlight a principal truth: our propensities are the structure blocks of our fate. Every little propensity, every day to day decision, fills in as a brushstroke in the terrific magnum opus of our lives. By assuming command over these decisions, by deliberately planning our propensities, we employ the ability to shape our future in arrangement with our most noteworthy goals.

This excursion of propensity change is a demonstration of the extraordinary versatility and strength of the human soul. It uncovers that change isn't just imaginable yet accessible for anybody able to focus on the cycle. The way may not generally be simple, and it will without a doubt be set apart by difficulties and misfortunes, yet the prizes of diligence are tremendous. Past the accomplishment of explicit objectives lies the more extensive victory of understanding our ability for development, learning, and reestablishment.

As you push ahead, let this book act as both an aide and a buddy in your continuous mission for individual greatness. Recollect that the specialty of propensity change is a powerful interaction, one that welcomes nonstop investigation, change, and refinement. Embrace this excursion with receptiveness, interest, and assurance, and know that with each propensity you effectively change, you step nearer to the fullest articulation of your true capacity.

May the extraordinary force of propensities enlighten your way, directing you towards a future overflowing with accomplishment, satisfaction, and a significant feeling of direction. The excursion ahead is yours to shape, each propensity in turn.

Appendix

Welcome to the Supplement, a clever buddy intended to help and enhance your process through propensity development and change. Here, you will find an organized assortment of apparatuses, readings, much of the time clarified some pressing issues, and formats custom-made to help you in exploring the intricacies of growing new propensities and changing existing ones. This exhaustive tool stash is planned to furnish you with down to earth help and more profound bits of knowledge as you leave on the way to self-awareness and efficiency.

Propensity Following and Arranging Apparatuses

Advanced Applications: Investigate applications like Habitica for gamifying your propensity arrangement, Todoist for coordinating and focusing on errands, and Daylio for state of mind following and recognizing designs in your propensities.

Actual Diaries: Think about putting resources into an actual propensity tracker or organizer, like the Projectile Diary, to customize your propensity following involvement in pen and paper.

Suggested Perusing and Assets

"Nuclear Propensities" by James Clear: Offers an extensive aide on the most proficient method to fabricate beneficial routines and break terrible ones, underlining the force of little changes.

"The Impact of trained instinct" by Charles Duhigg: Gives experiences into the study of propensity arrangement in our lives, organizations, and social orders.

"Attitude: The New Brain research of Progress" via Ditty S. Dweck: Investigates the idea of "attitude" and what our convictions about ourselves can mean for each part of our lives, including propensity change.

FAQs about Propensity Development and Change

What amount of time does it require to frame another propensity?

While the usually refered to period is 21 days, research proposes it can shift generally contingent upon the individual and the propensity, going from 18 to 254 days.

Is it conceivable to improve on various propensities without a moment's delay? While it's conceivable, zeroing in on each propensity change in turn is in many cases more compelling to keep away from overpower and improve the probability of achievement.

How would it be advisable for me to respond on the off chance that I break faith on another propensity? Perceive that misfortunes are essential for the interaction. Think about what prompted the lose the faith, change your arrangement if necessary, and delicately guide yourself in the groove again.

Layouts for Propensity Following and Arranging

Everyday Propensity Tracker: Make a basic network for every month, with propensities recorded down the side and days of the month across the top. Verify or variety in every day you effectively complete a propensity.

Week after week Propensity Organizer: Gap your week into days, and allocate explicit propensities to explicit times or signals every day. Incorporate space for considering victories and regions for development at the week's end.

Objective and Propensity Arrangement Worksheet: Begin with your drawn out objectives, then work in reverse to distinguish which propensities can assist you with accomplishing these objectives. For each propensity, note the prompt, everyday practice, and award.

This Index is intended to be a living piece of your excursion, developing as you find what instruments and assets best help your exceptional way to excelling at propensity. Whether you favor computerized devices for their benefit and bits of knowledge or the material experience of pen and paper, the main step is to begin. Utilize these assets as an establishment, and feel free to them as you develop and realize what turns out best for you.